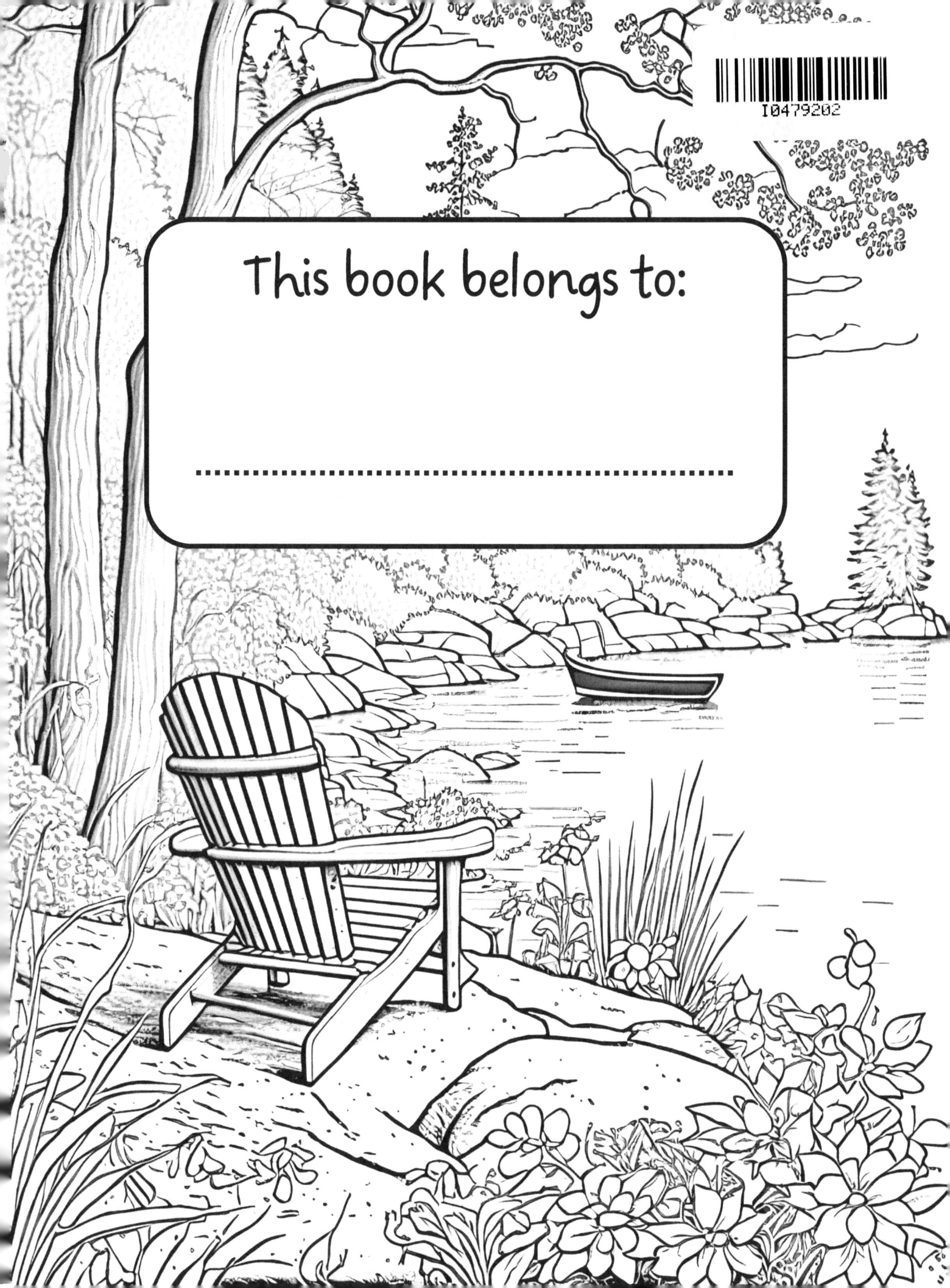

This book belongs to:

....

A rustic porch, a quiet morn,
My armchair waits, as day is born,
Birds on wing, their music sweet,
In this haven of summer heat.

Idyllic Retreats

A Summer-Themed Coloring Book with Poems to Inspire

Welcome to "Idyllic Retreats - A Summer-Themed Coloring Book with Poems to Inspire," where we invite you to embark on a journey to the most enchanting and relaxing summer landscapes. This unique coloring book brings together beautifully crafted coloring pages and heartfelt poems, allowing you to escape the hustle and bustle of everyday life and immerse yourself in the serenity of idyllic summer scenes.

Picture yourself lounging in a cozy armchair, nestled in a sun-dappled corner of a serene landscape, sipping on a refreshing glass of lemonade as you lose yourself in the gentle sway of the trees and the soothing melody of birdsong. Each coloring page in this book has been meticulously designed to capture the essence of a perfect summer day, with comfortable armchairs nestled in tranquil settings that beckon you to unwind and relax.

To further enhance your coloring experience, each page is accompanied by a thought-provoking and inspiring poem that perfectly complements the scene. Let the verses transport you to a peaceful world, where the warmth of the sun and the gentle rustle of leaves whisper sweet nothings to your soul.

Whether you're an experienced coloring enthusiast or just looking for a way to de-stress and recharge, "Idyllic Retreats" offers something for everyone. So grab your favorite coloring tools and let the vivid hues of summer inspire your creative spirit. As you color your way through these tranquil landscapes, may you find the peace and serenity that your heart desires.

Sun-dappled meadows, a gentle breeze,
In my armchair, I sit at ease,
Nature's symphony, whispers soft,
In this idyllic summer loft.

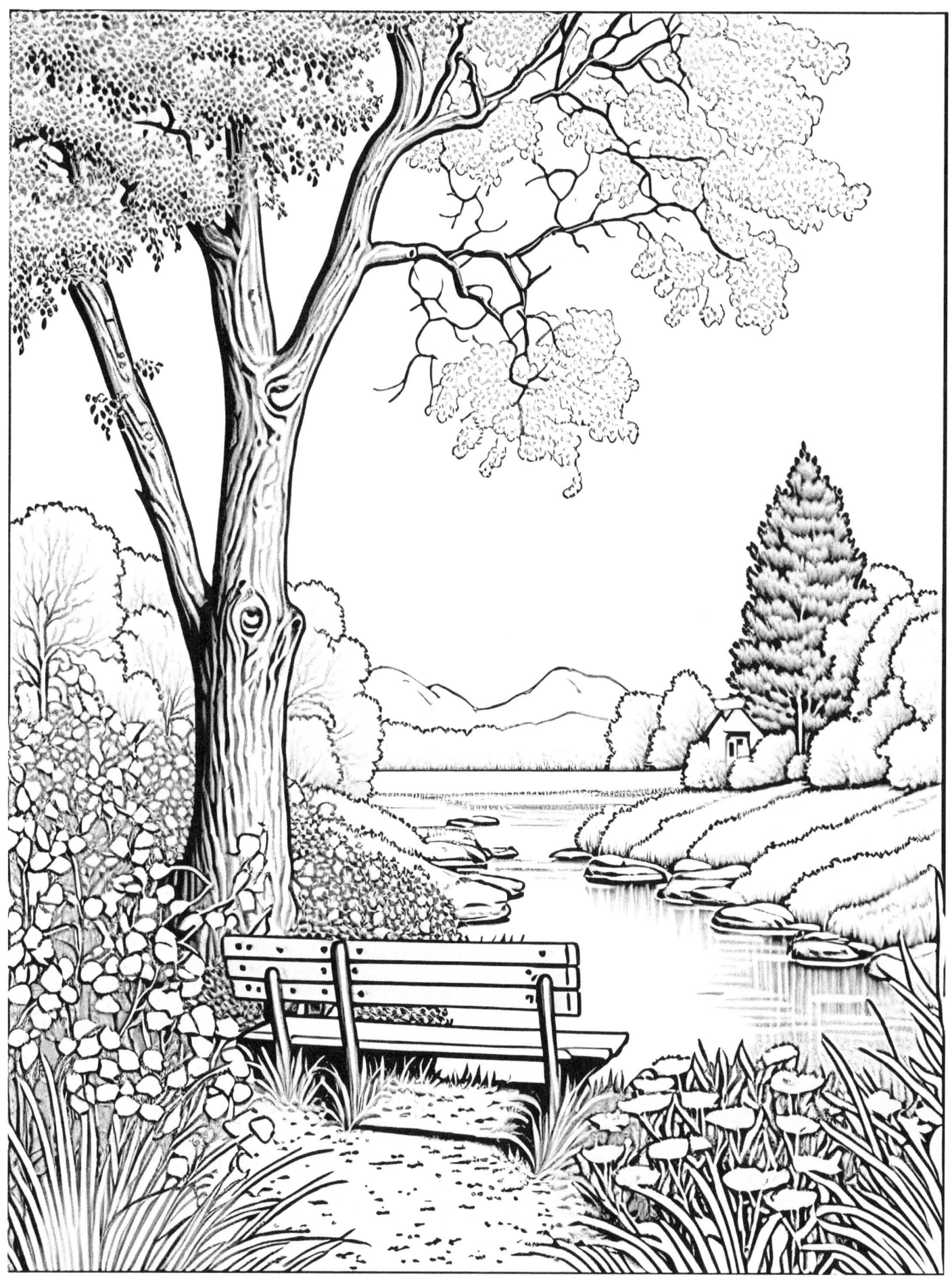

Beneath the willow, shadows play,
A quiet refuge, where I lay,
Armchair cradling, dreams take flight,
In golden hues of warm sunlight.

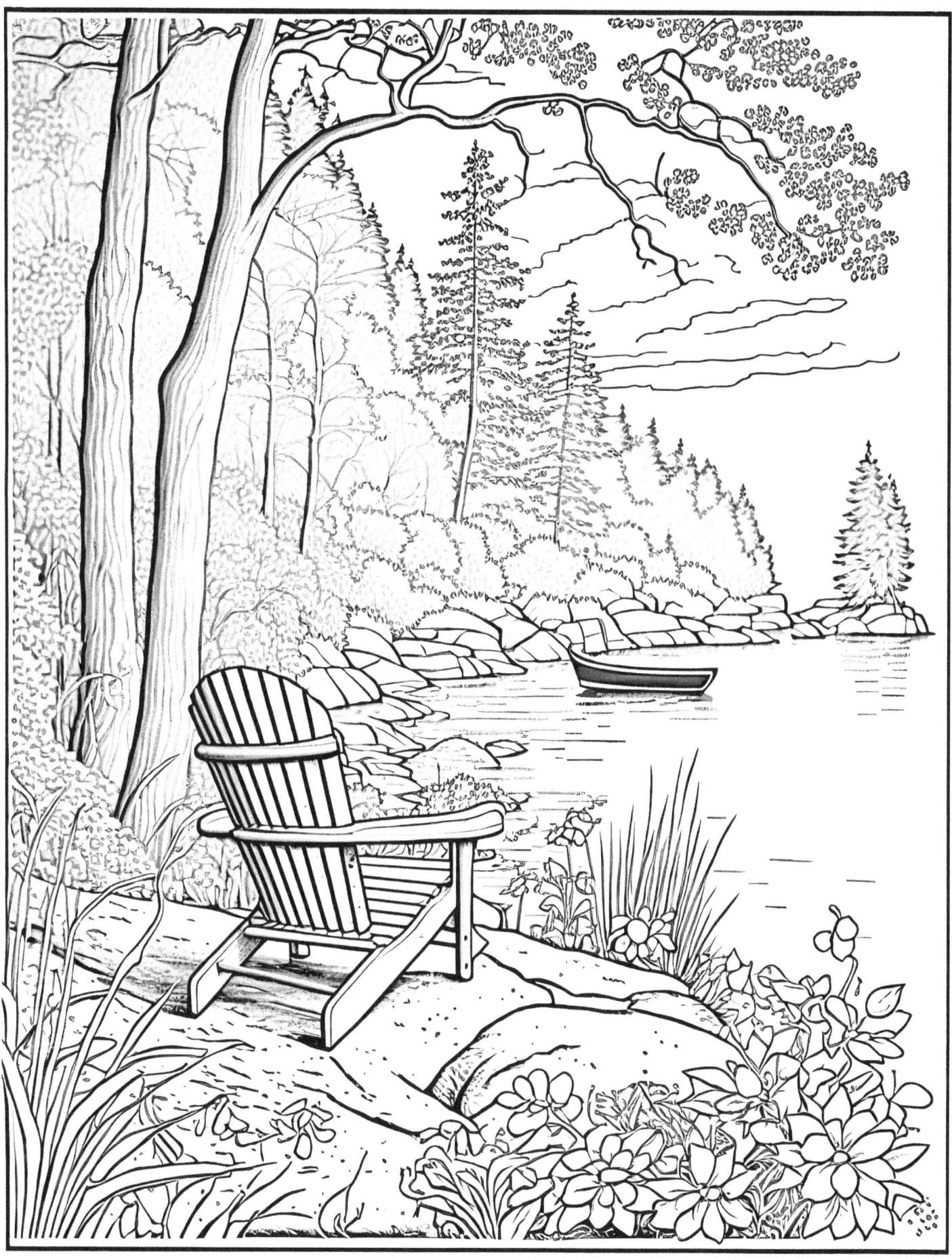

By the lakeside, serenity found,
An armchair waits on soft, green ground,
Ripples on water, a calming sight,
In this sanctuary bathed in light.

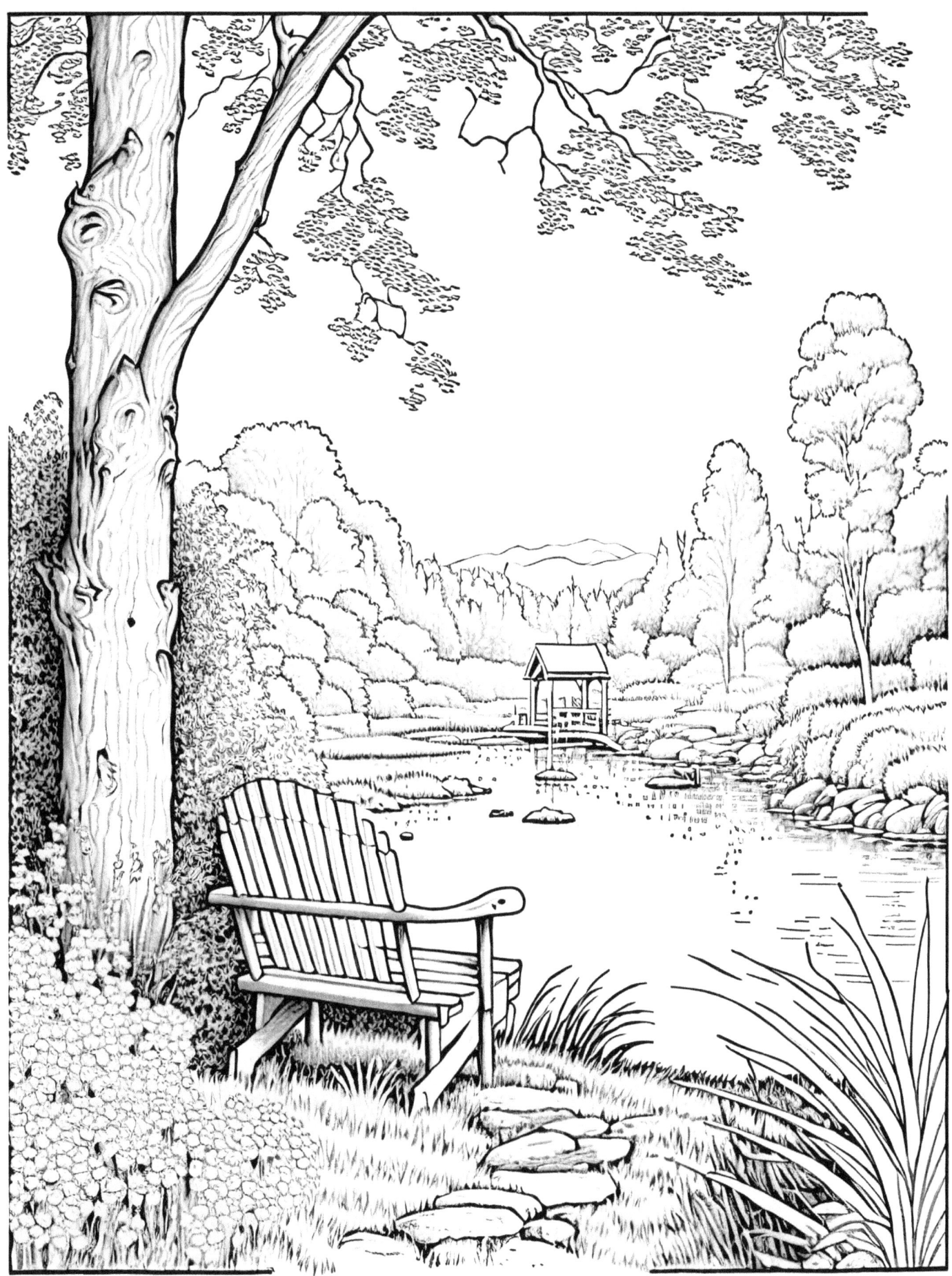

The scent of roses fills the air,
A garden path leads to a chair,
A place to rest, and thoughts to clear,
In this haven where peace is near.

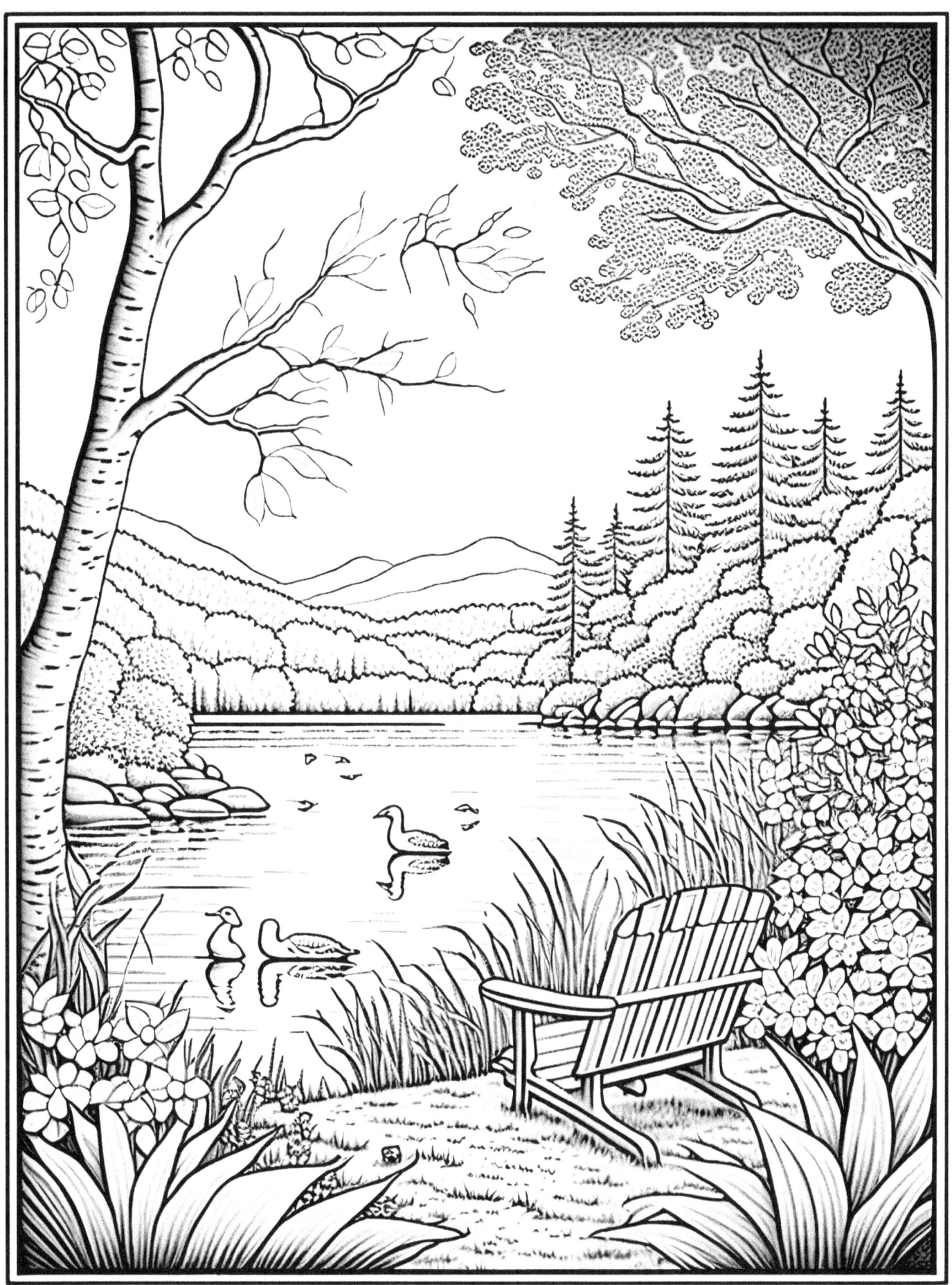

A cozy nook, beneath an oak,
A cherished book, a heart unbroke,
In my armchair, I find reprieve,
As nature's tapestry weaves.

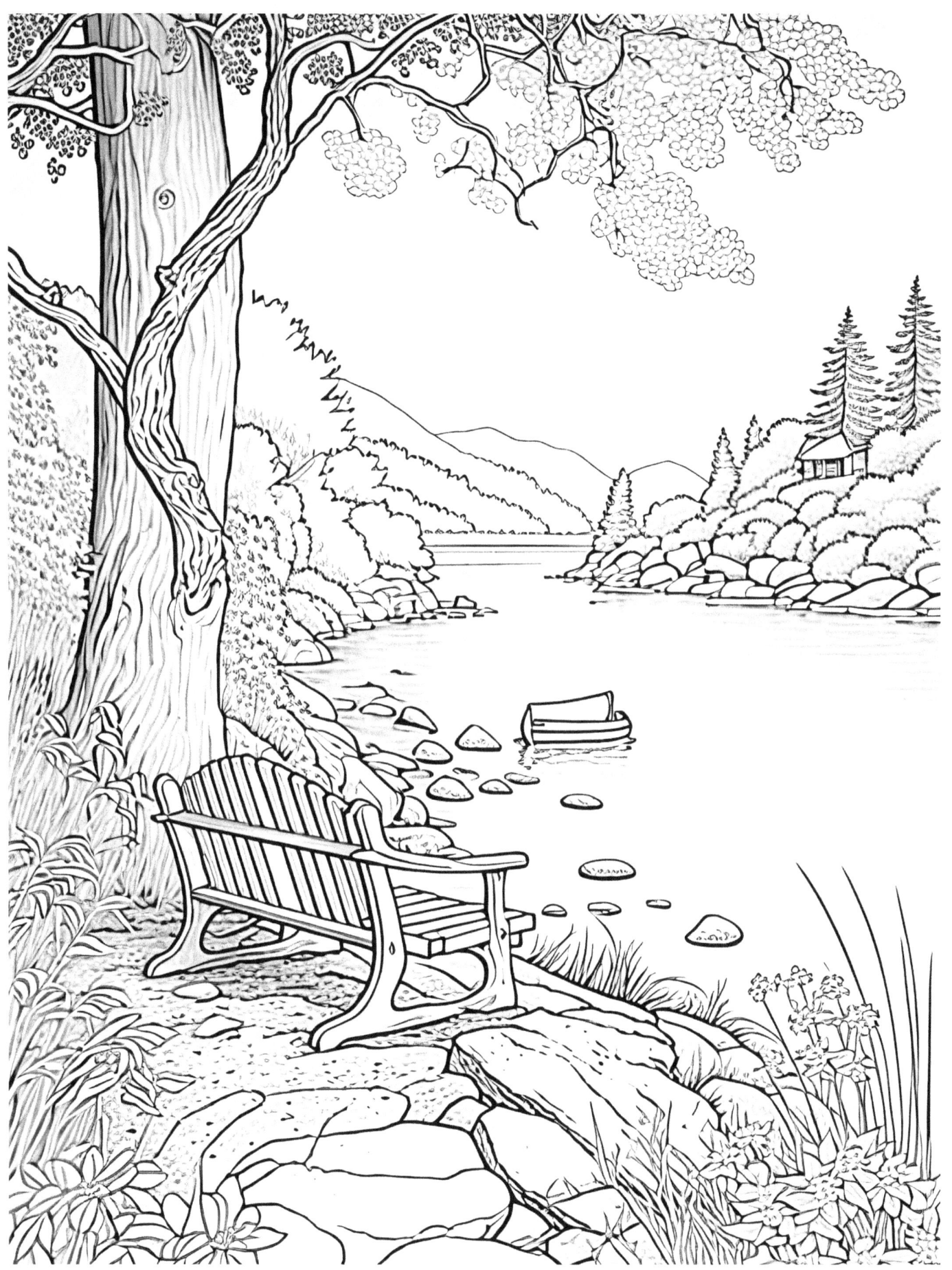

Mountain vistas, endless skies,
A quiet spot, where beauty lies,
An armchair nestled in the scene,
An invitation to daydream.

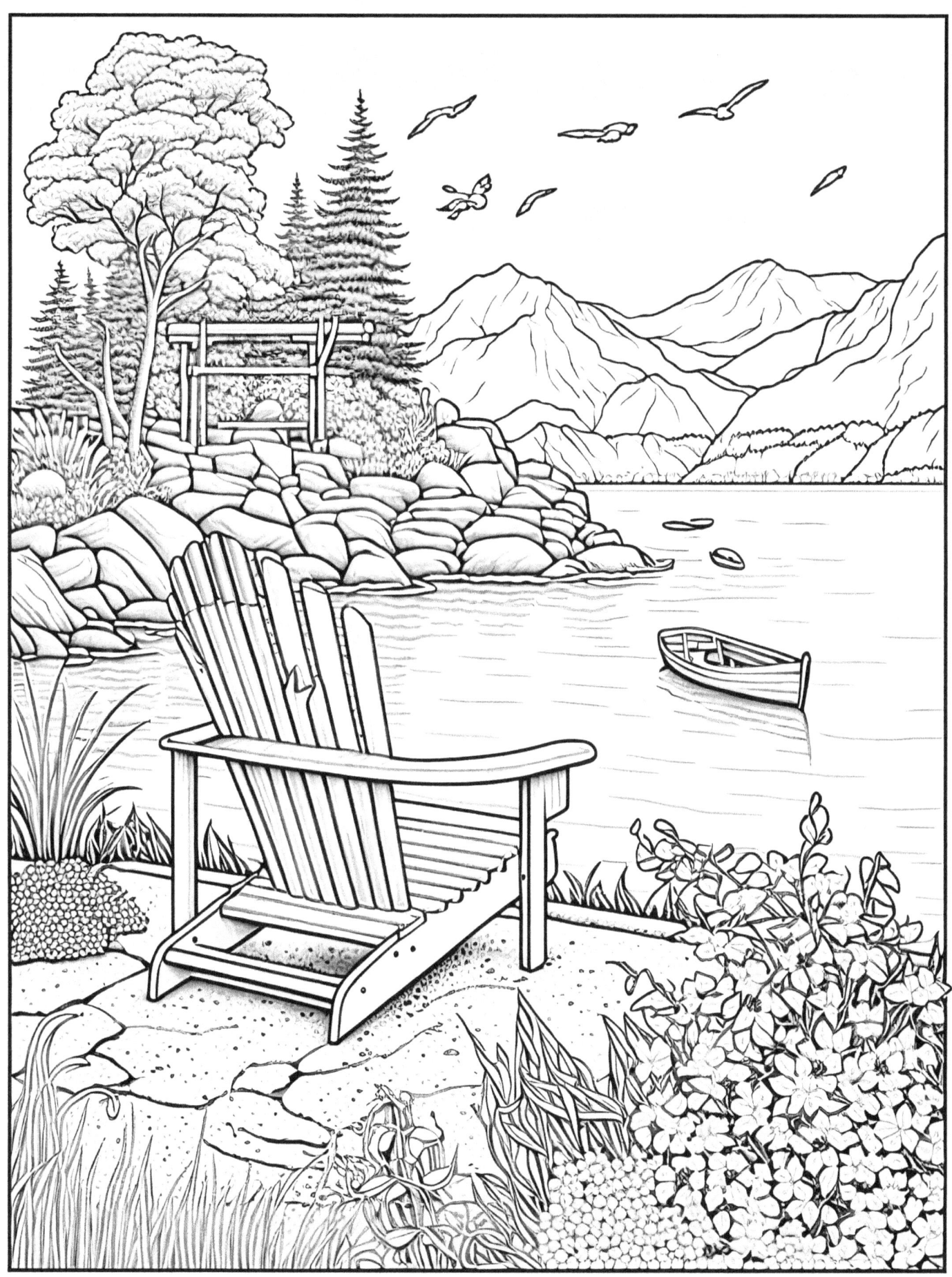

A hidden glen, a secret place,
My armchair rests with quiet grace,
In dappled shade, my thoughts can roam,
A sanctuary to call my own.

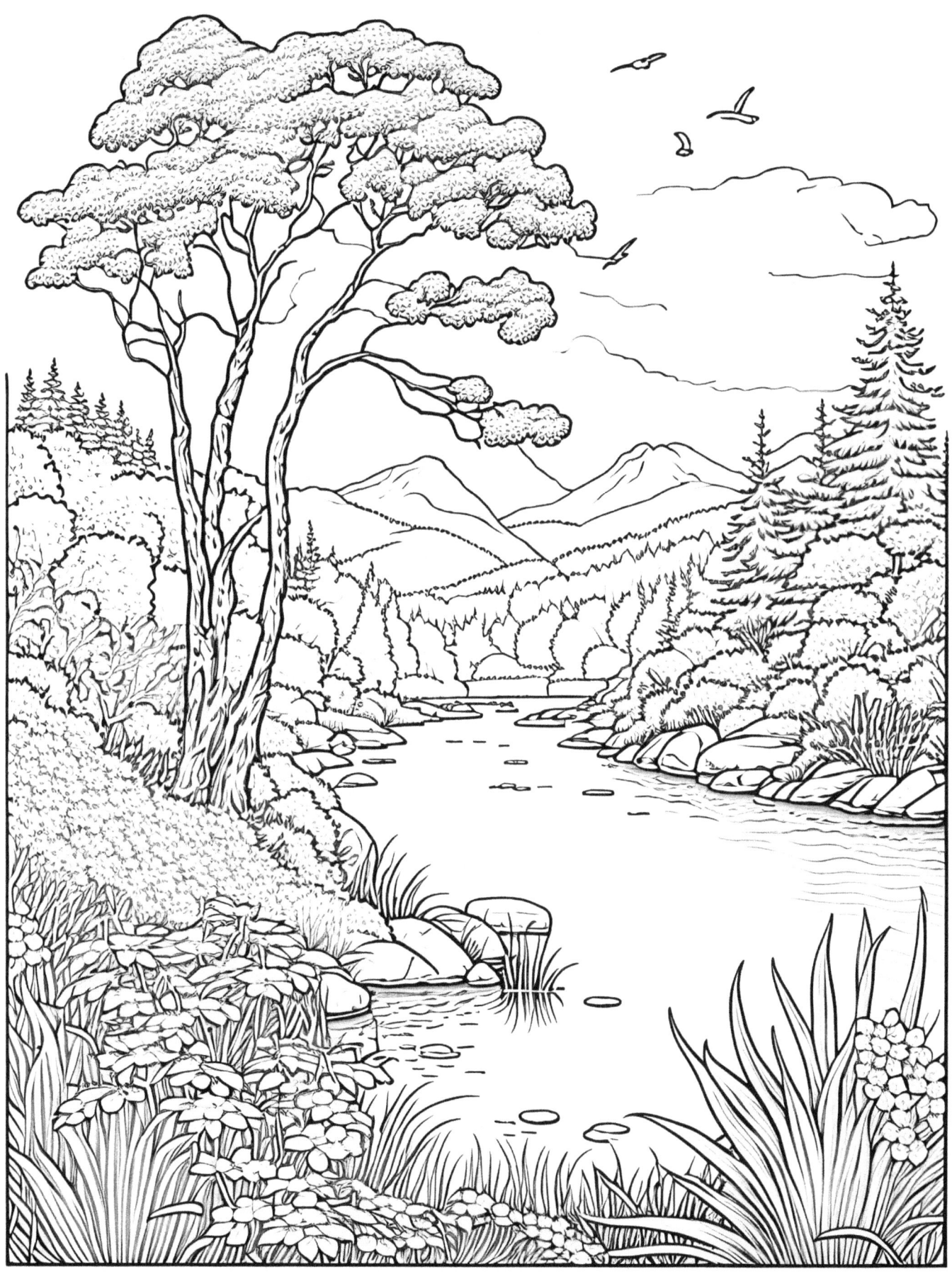

The ocean's lull, a gentle call,
A sandy beach, my chair enthralled,
The ebbing tide, a soothing balm,
In this seascape of endless calm.

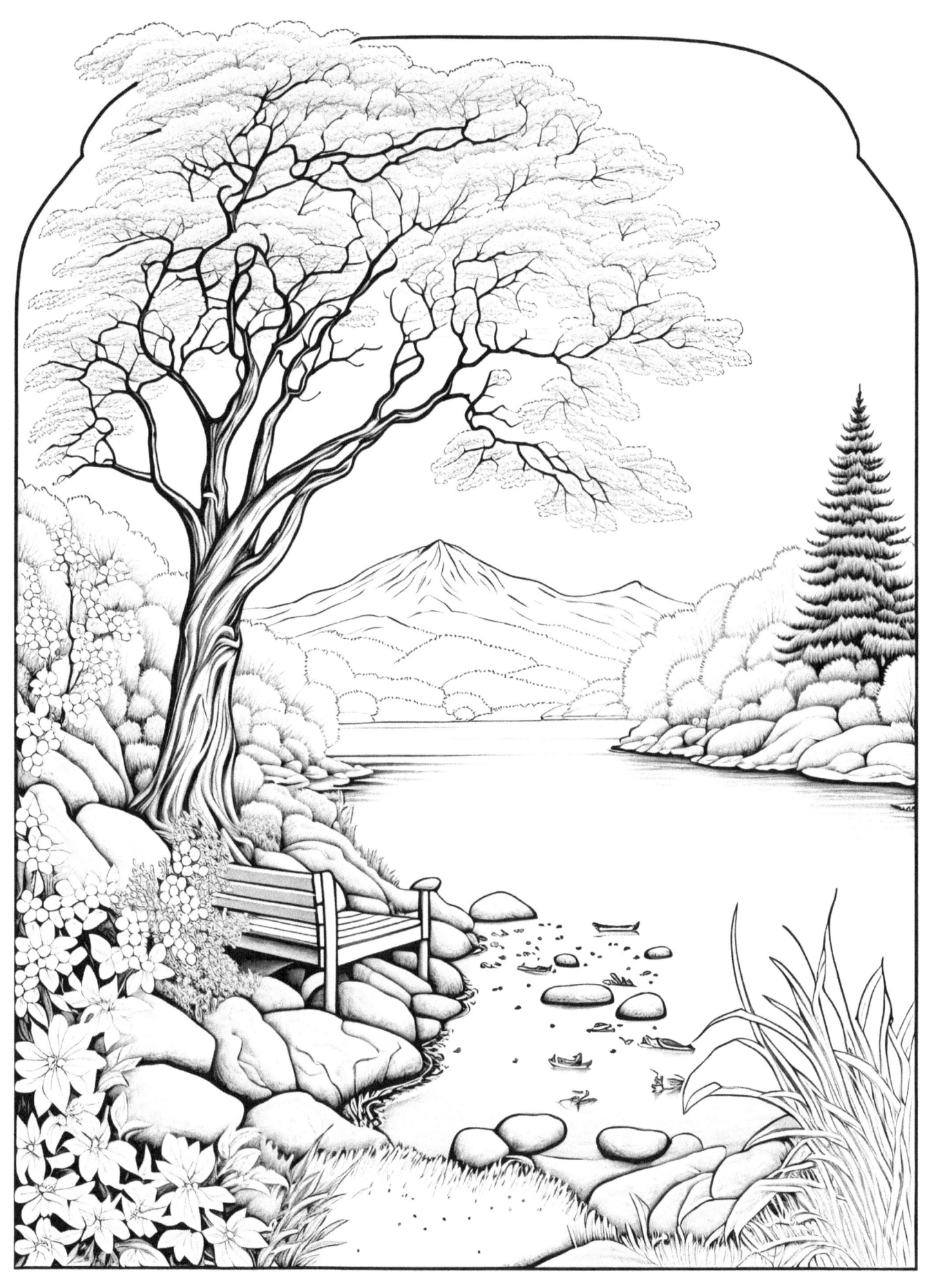

A woodland grove, alive with song,
My armchair beckons, all day long,
With every leaf, a story told,
Of summer days, and love untold.

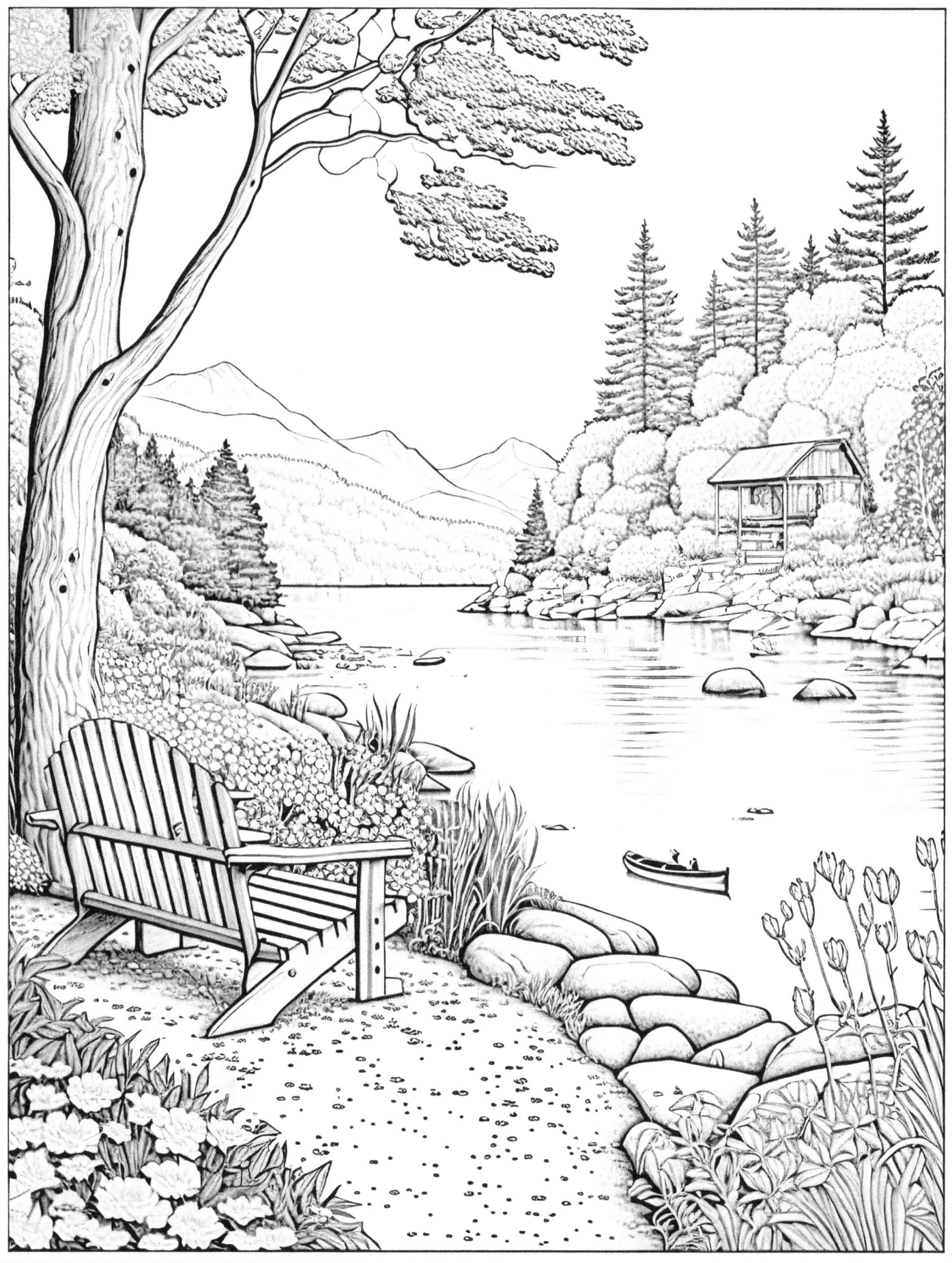

A fragrant meadow, blooms in tow,
An armchair waits, as breezes blow,
In quiet repose, my soul takes flight,
In this paradise of summer light.

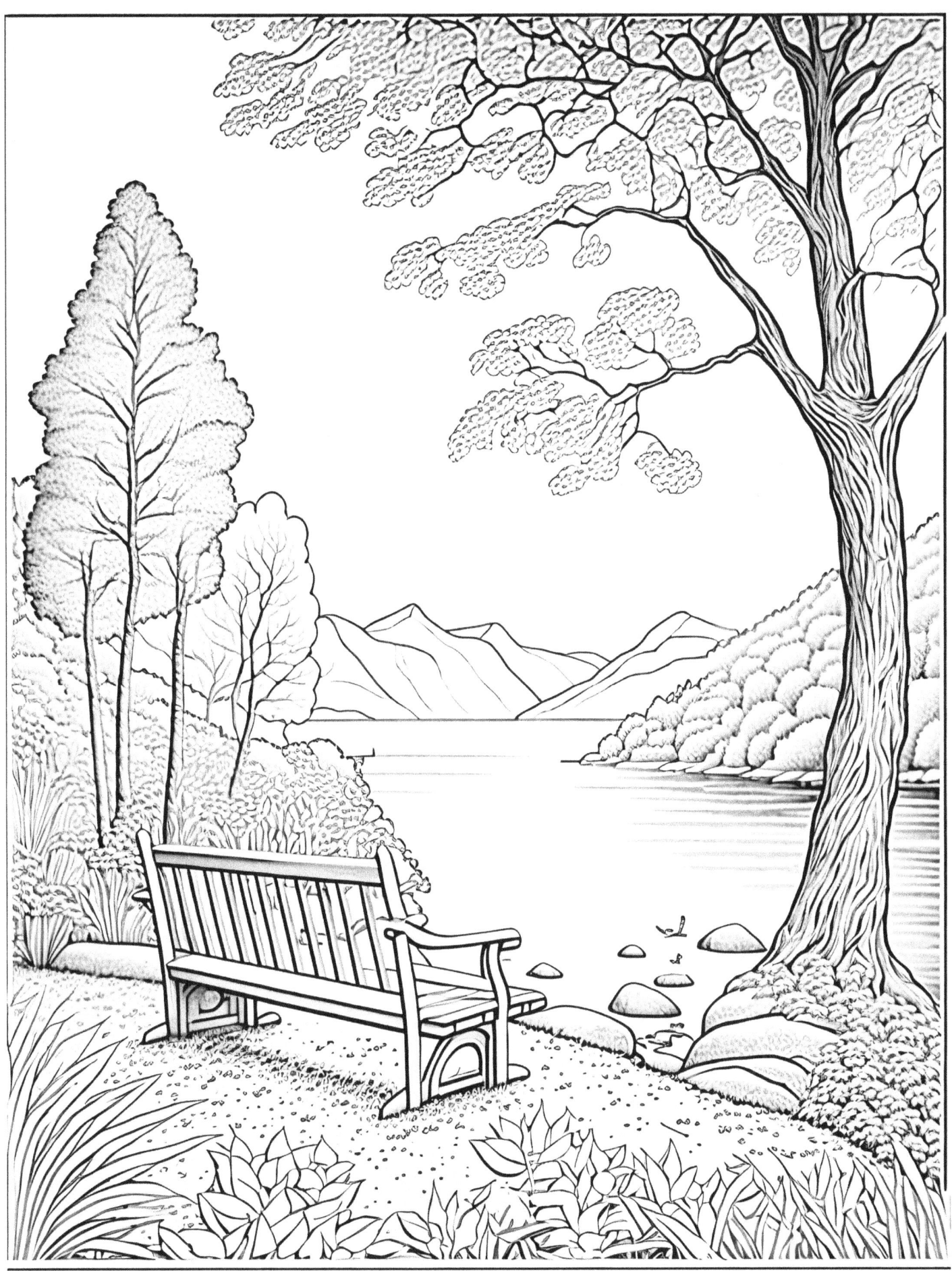

Cascading falls, a sight to see,
In my armchair, I sit carefree,
The water's dance, a sweet refrain,
Washing away life's fleeting pain.

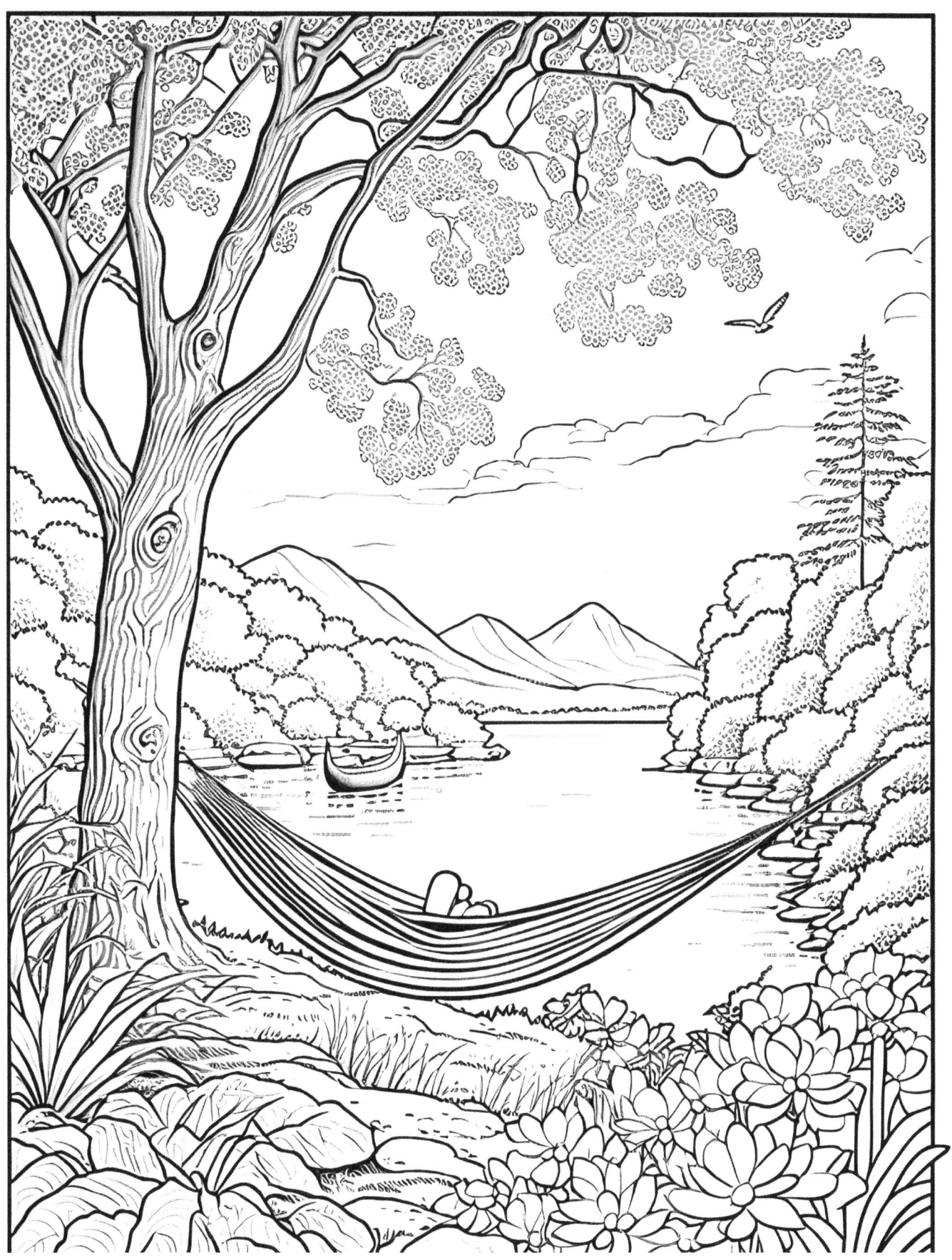

A rustic porch, a quiet morn,
My armchair waits, as day is born,
Birds on wing, their music sweet,
In this haven of summer heat.

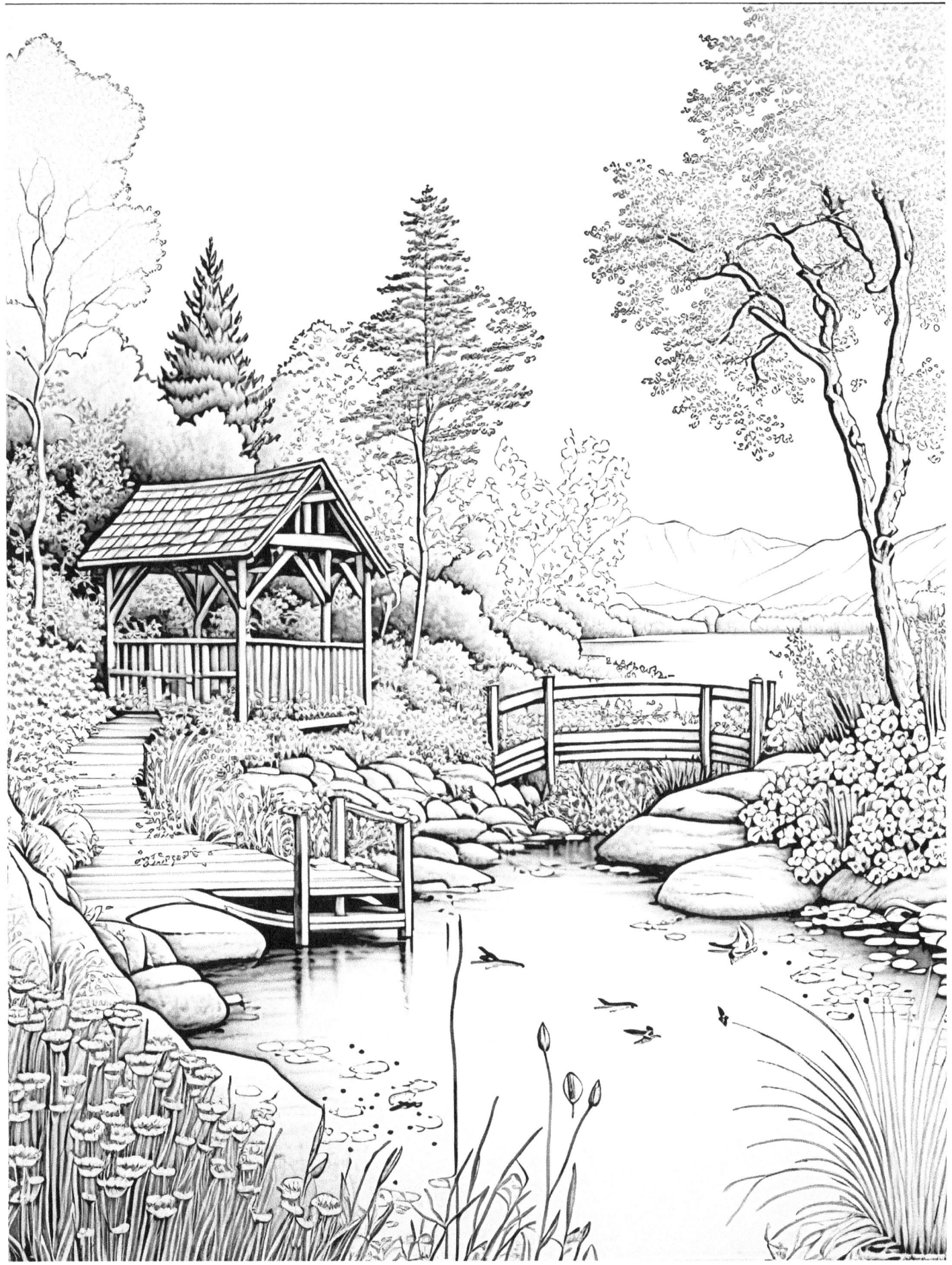

Twilight's glow, a soft embrace,
A secret garden, my resting place,
In my armchair, the stars align,
A summer night, forever mine.

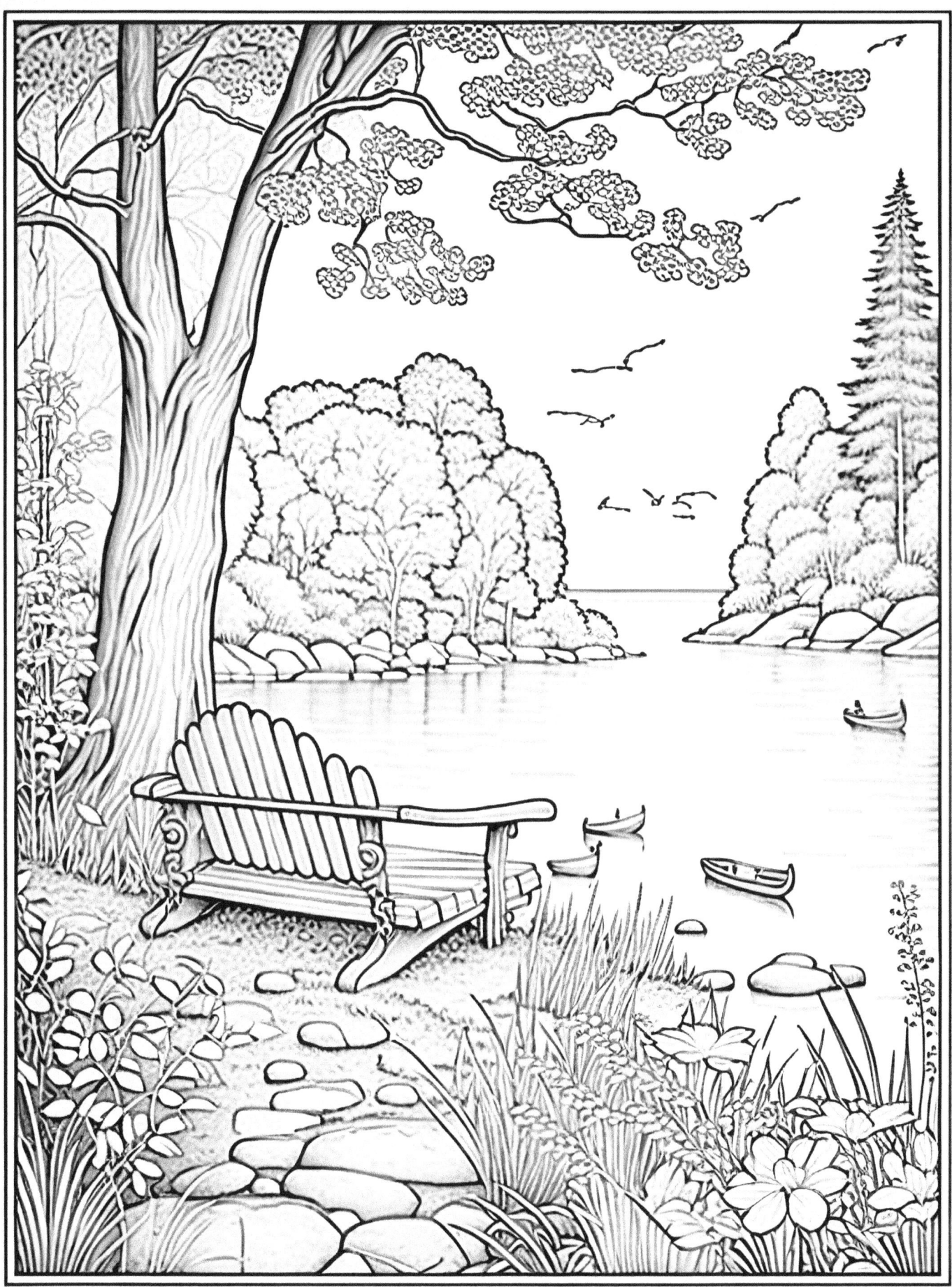

A sunlit glade, a butterfly's dance,
My armchair waits for a quiet chance,
To rest, reflect, and find release,
In this haven of endless peace.

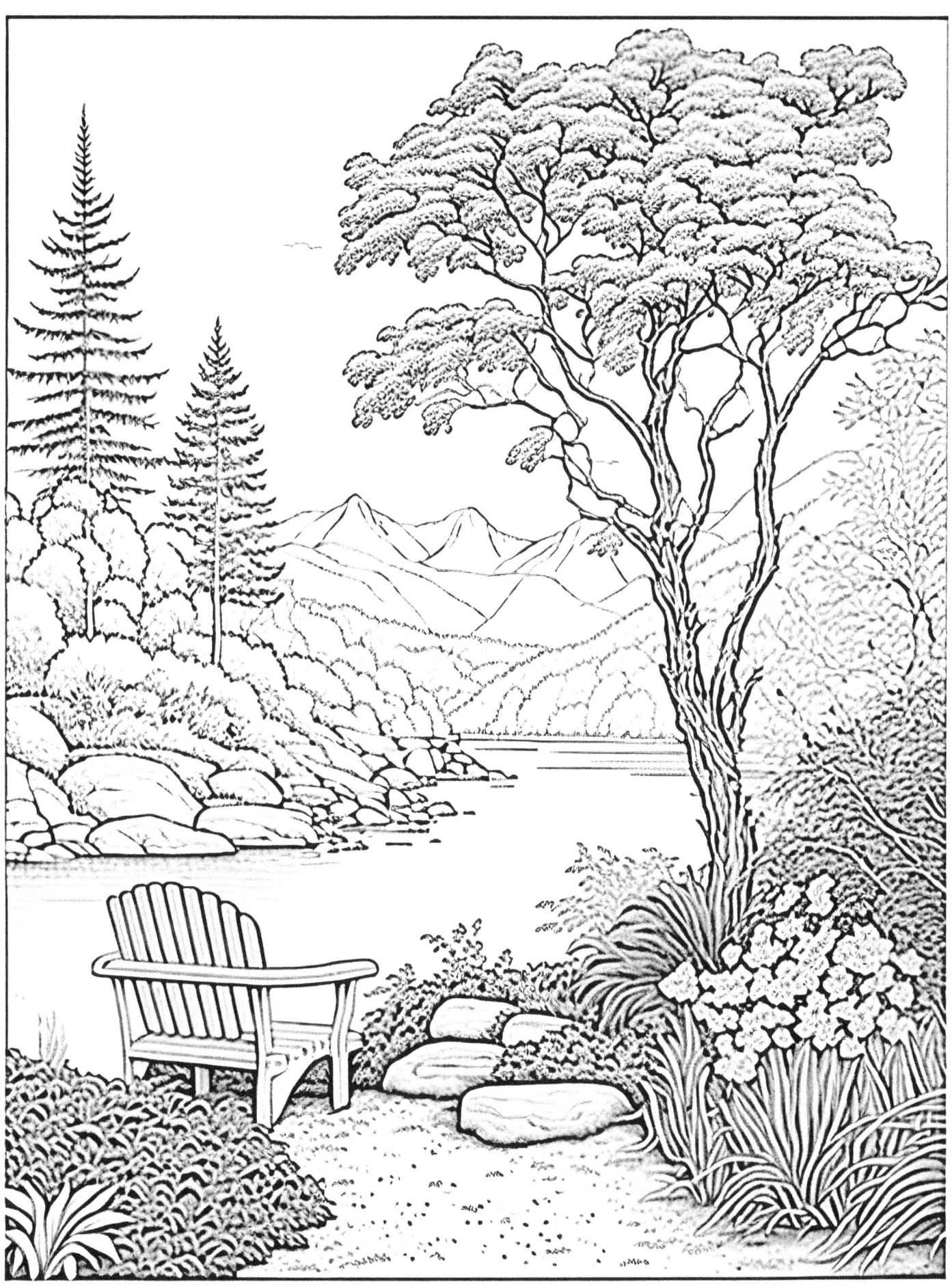

A river's bend, a calm retreat,
An armchair calls, a soothing seat,
The water's song, a lullaby,
In this sanctuary, time stands by.

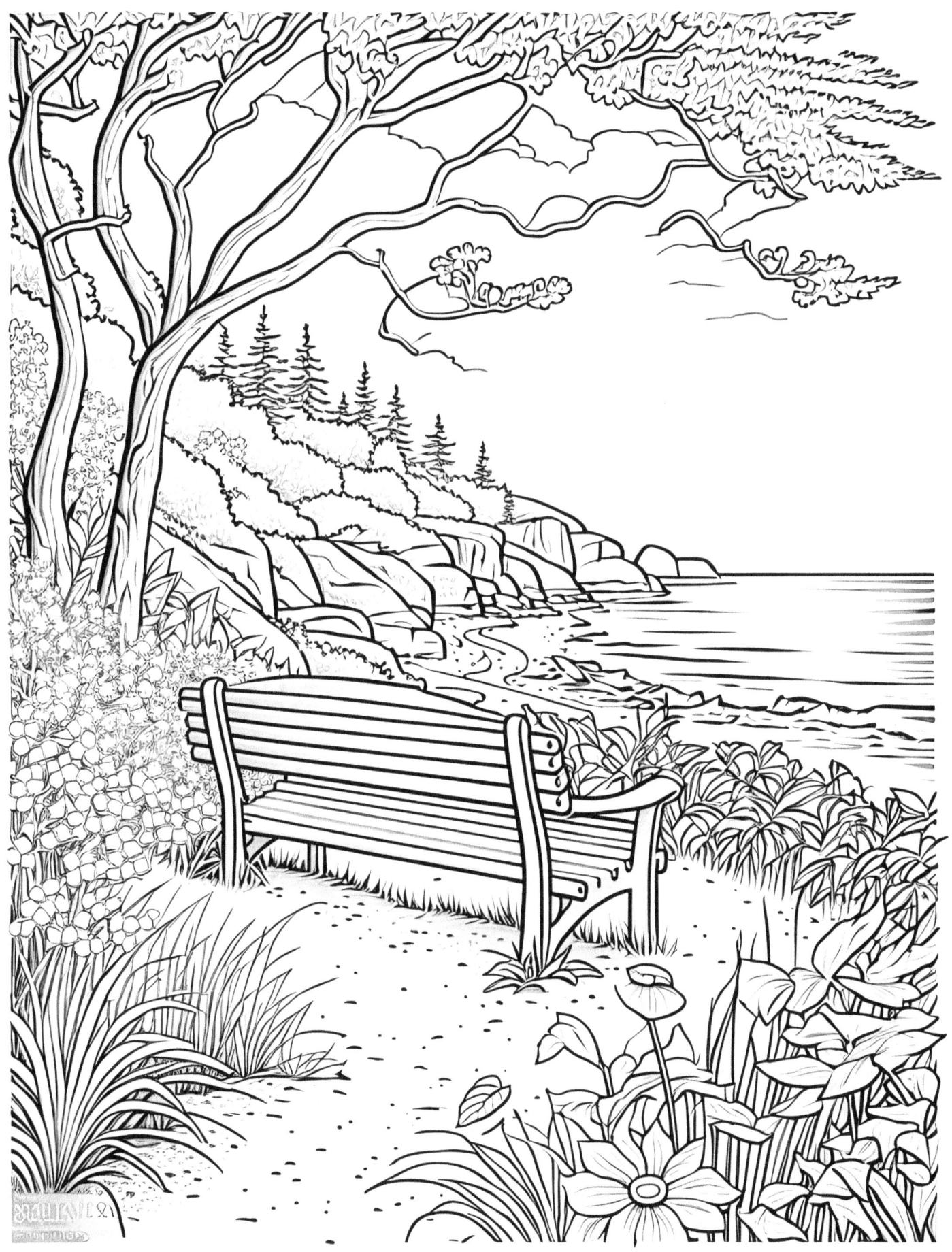

A poppy field, a vivid hue,
An armchair waits, a perfect view,
In this landscape, my heart doth sing,
Of summer's joy and everything.

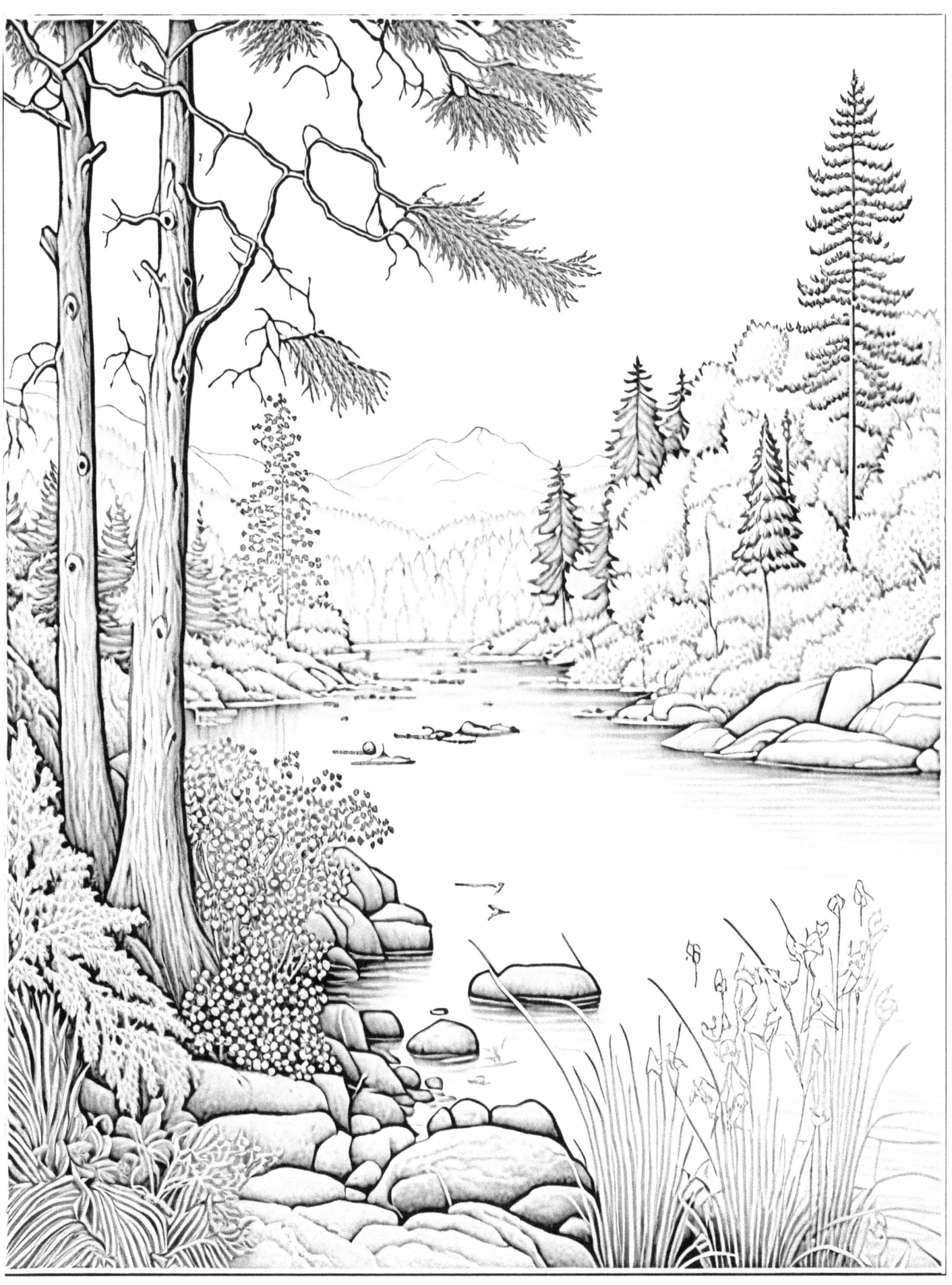

An orchard's shade, a fruit so sweet,
A place to rest, my chair replete,
Sunbeams dance, and shadows play,
In this refuge where I can stay.

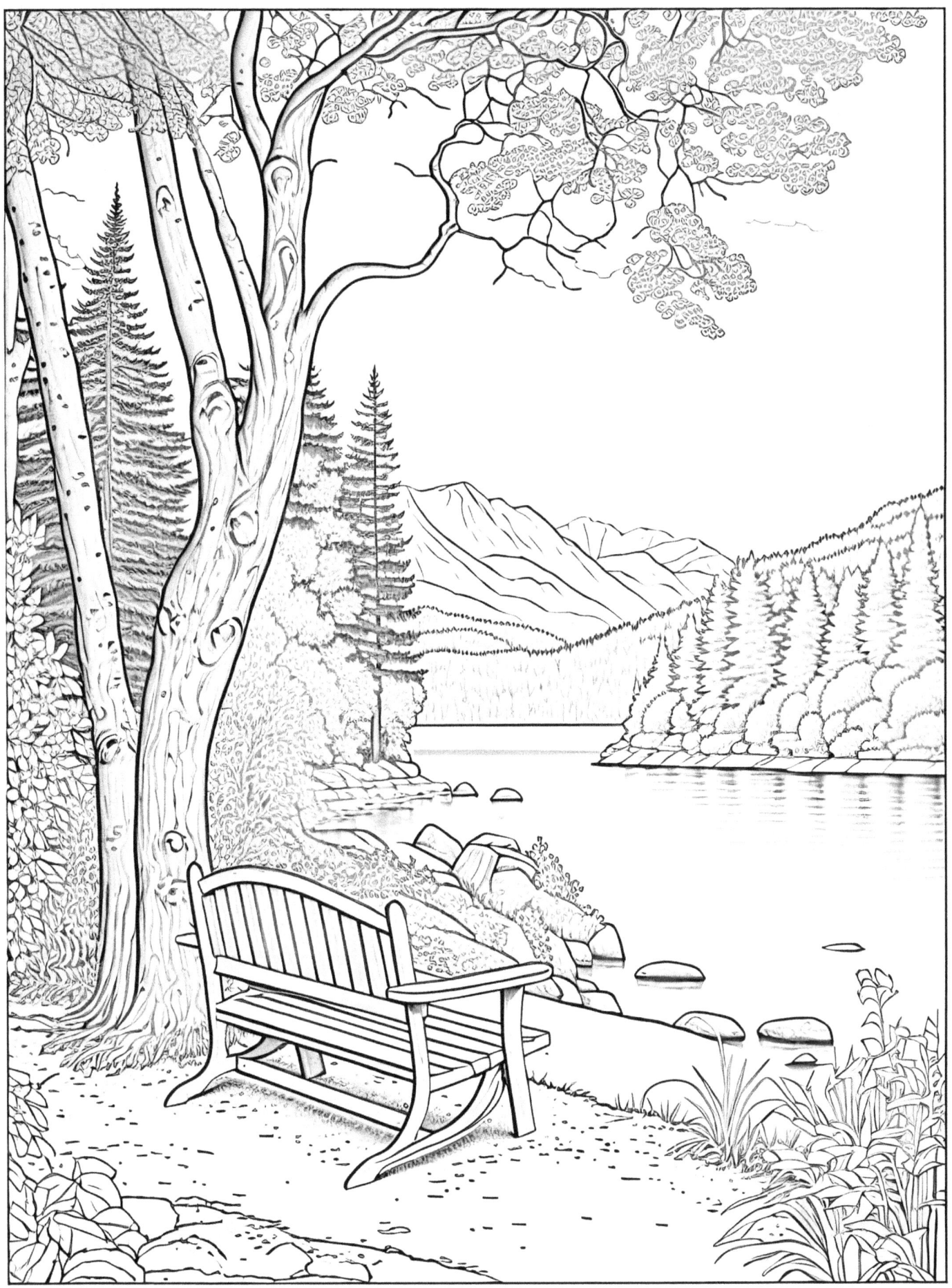

A lighthouse stands, a sentinel,
My armchair waits, a safe citadel,
The sea's embrace, a love so pure,
In this haven, my heart endures.

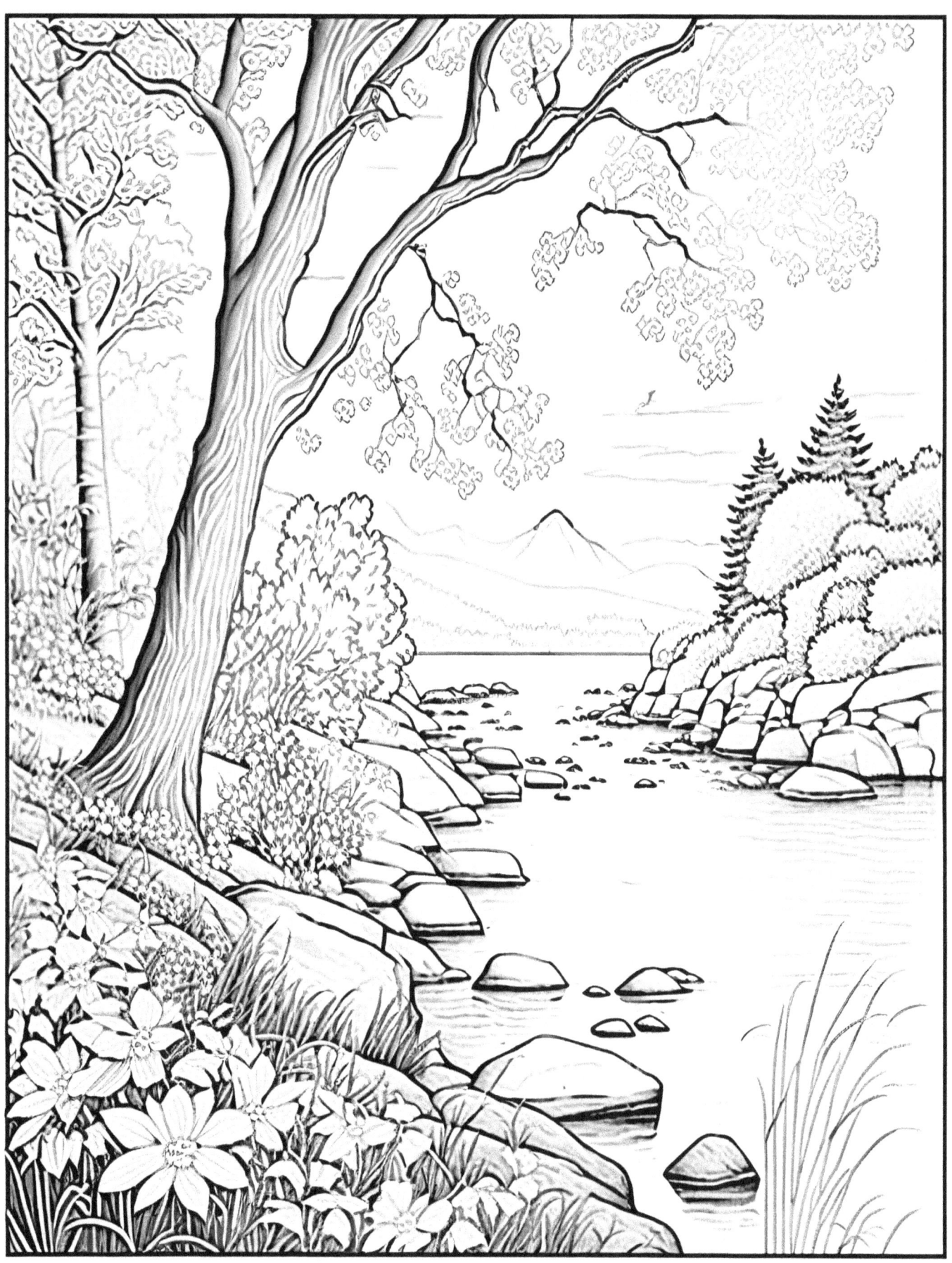

A vineyard's bounty, a rustic charm,
An armchair waits, a quiet calm,
Grapes ripen, as sunshine streams,
In this paradise of daydreams.

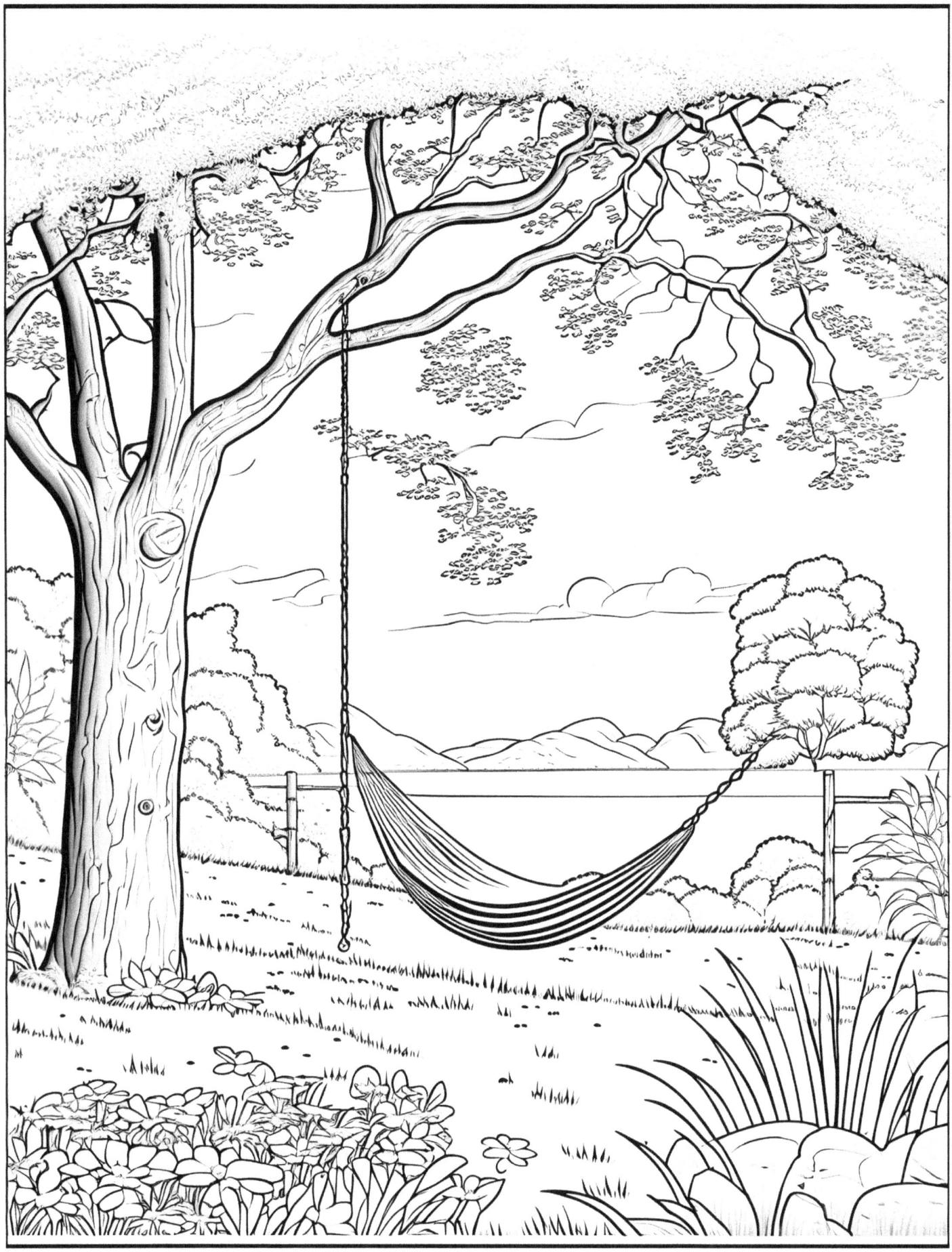

A quiet lane, a sleepy town,
An armchair waits, as sun goes down,
In this corner, I find my rest,
A tranquil haven, I feel blessed.

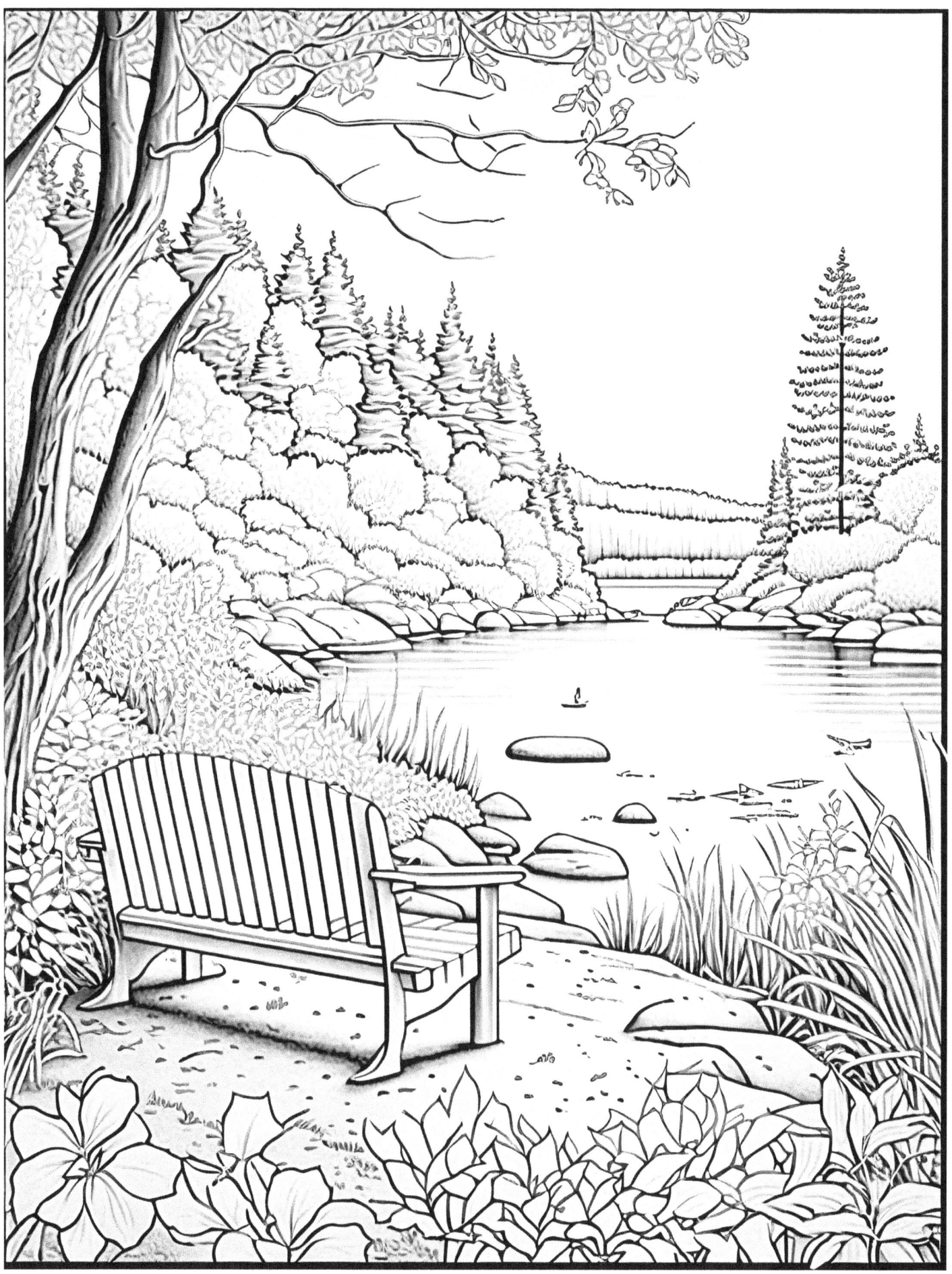

A meadow's edge, a painter's scene,
An armchair waits, in colors serene,
Wildflowers sway, in summer's glow,
In this haven, where dreams can grow.

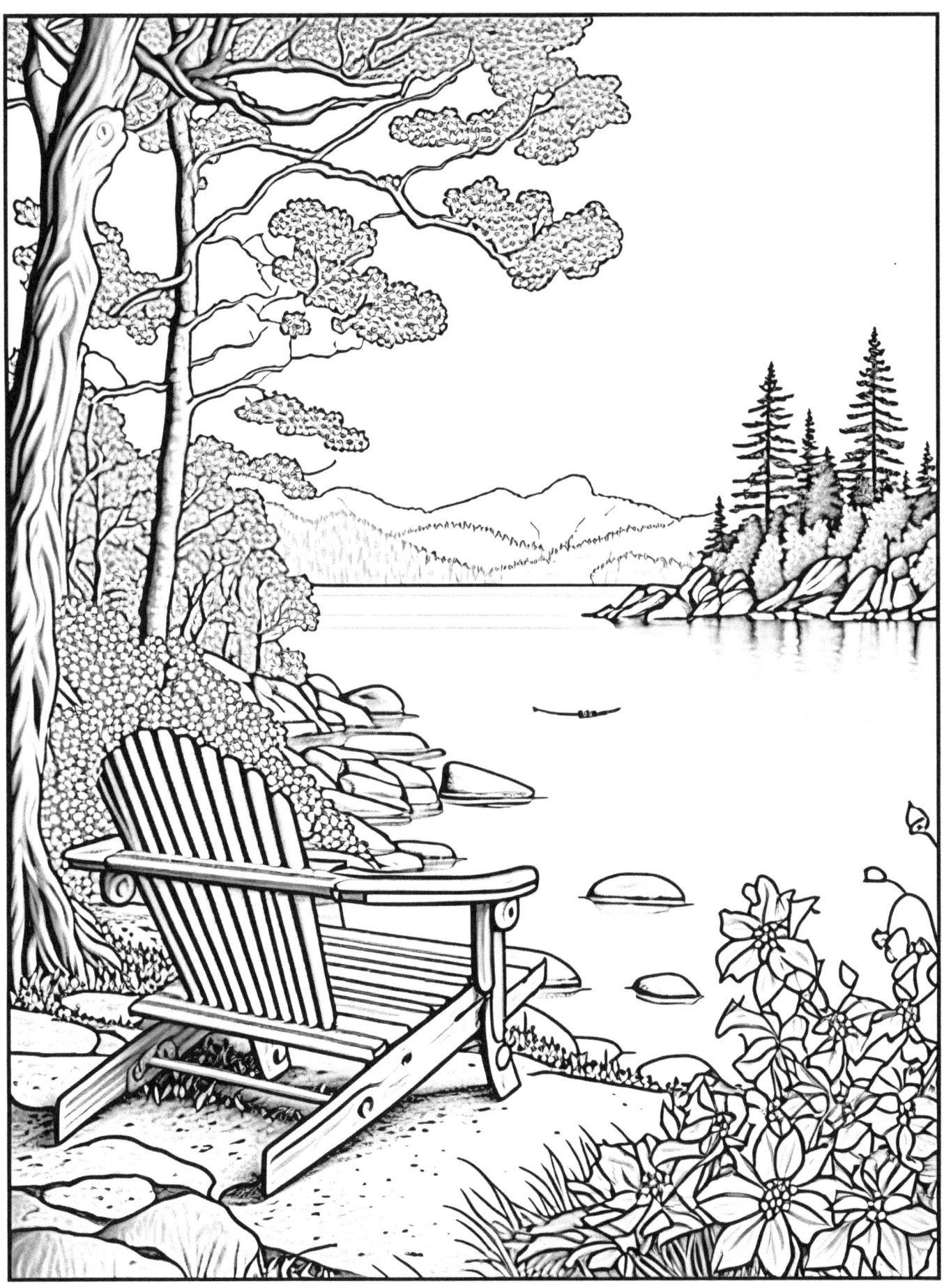

A mountain peak, a world so vast,
An armchair waits, as time drifts past,
Endless skies, a heart set free,
In this landscape, I find tranquility.

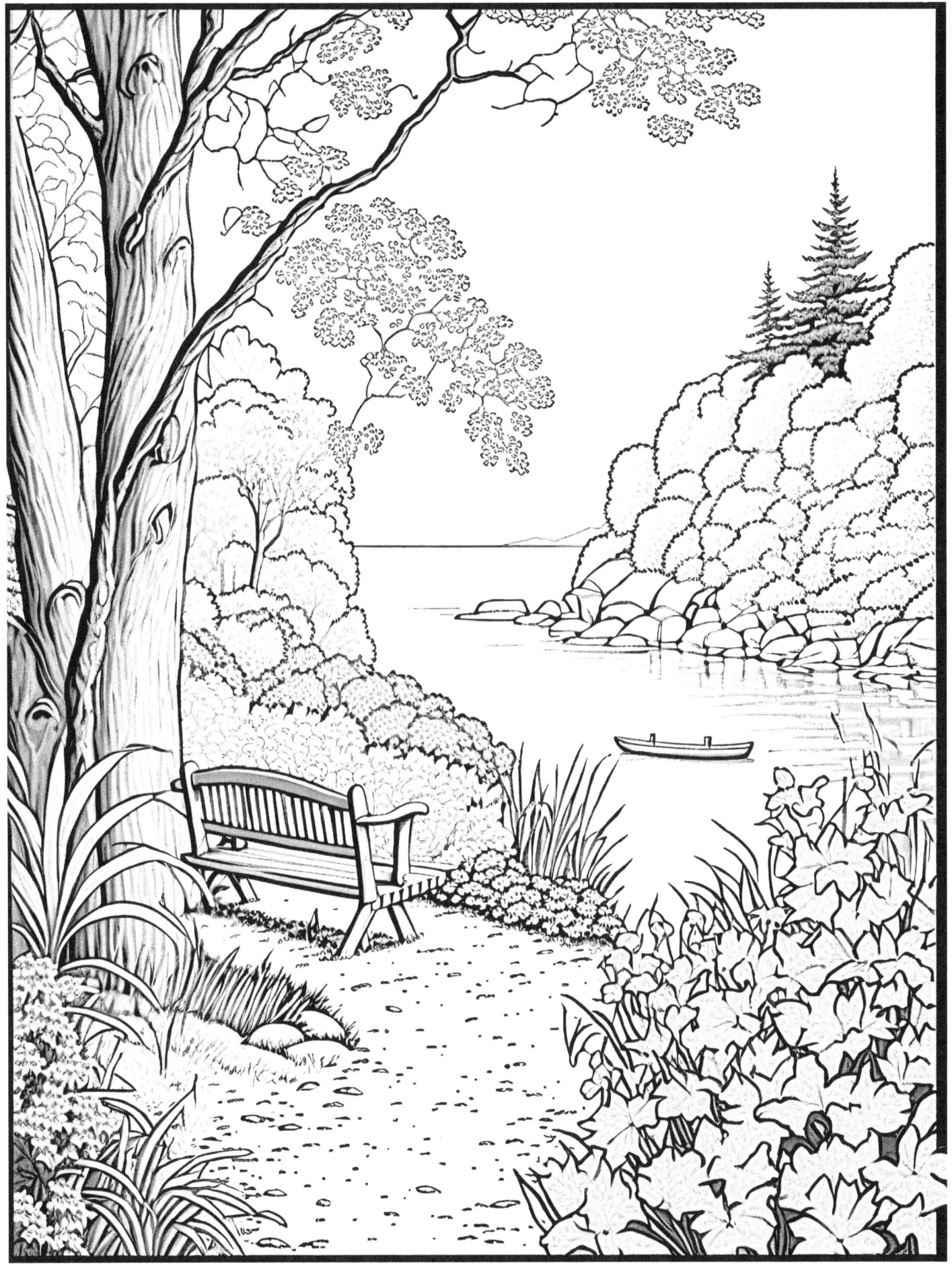

A rocky shore, a sunset's grace,
An armchair waits, in a quiet space,
Waves caress, the world so still,
In this seascape, my soul can thrill.

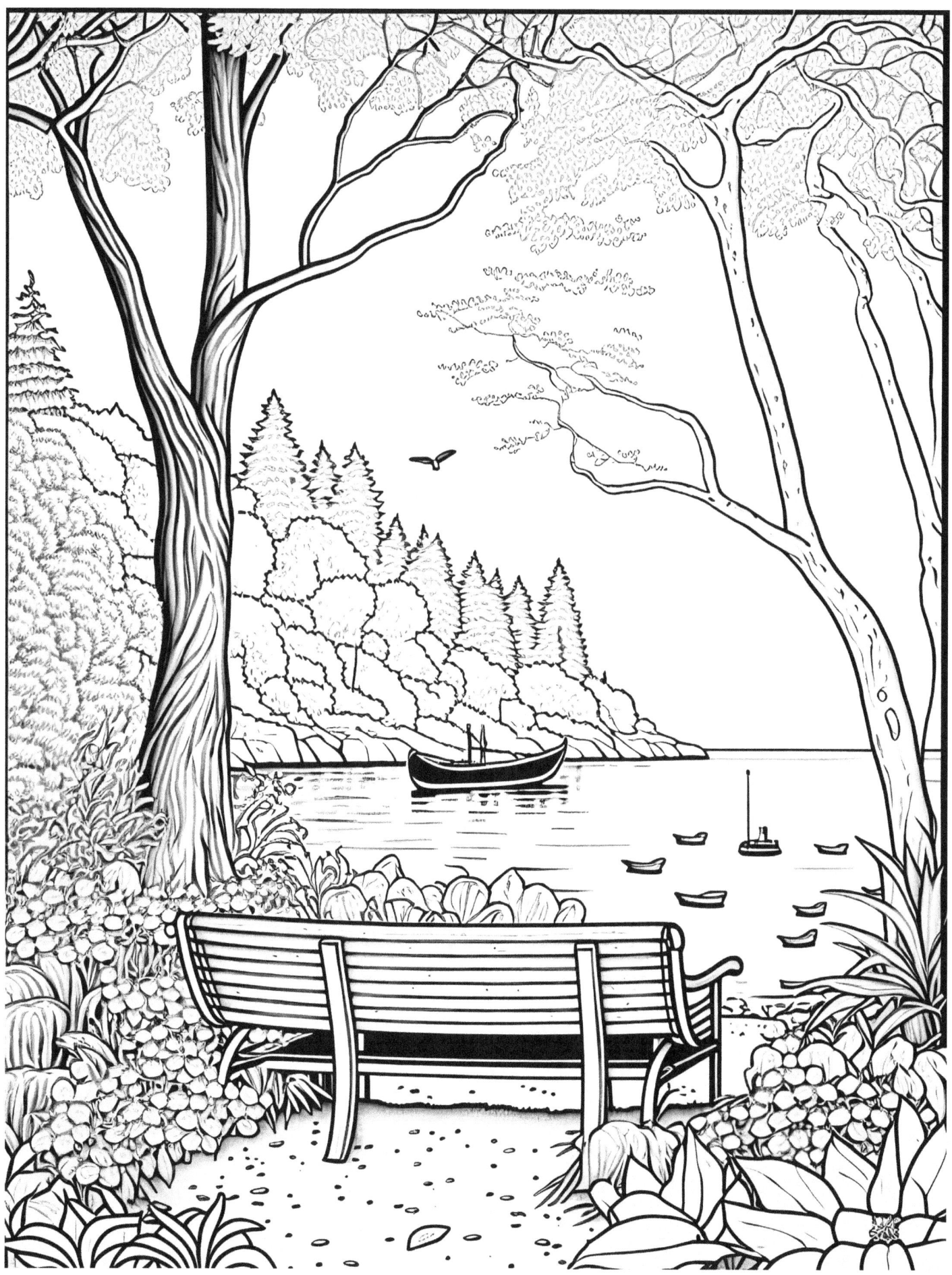

A hidden cove, a pirate's dream,
An armchair waits, by a moonlit stream,
In this haven, my thoughts can wander,
As summer's beauty, I sit and ponder.

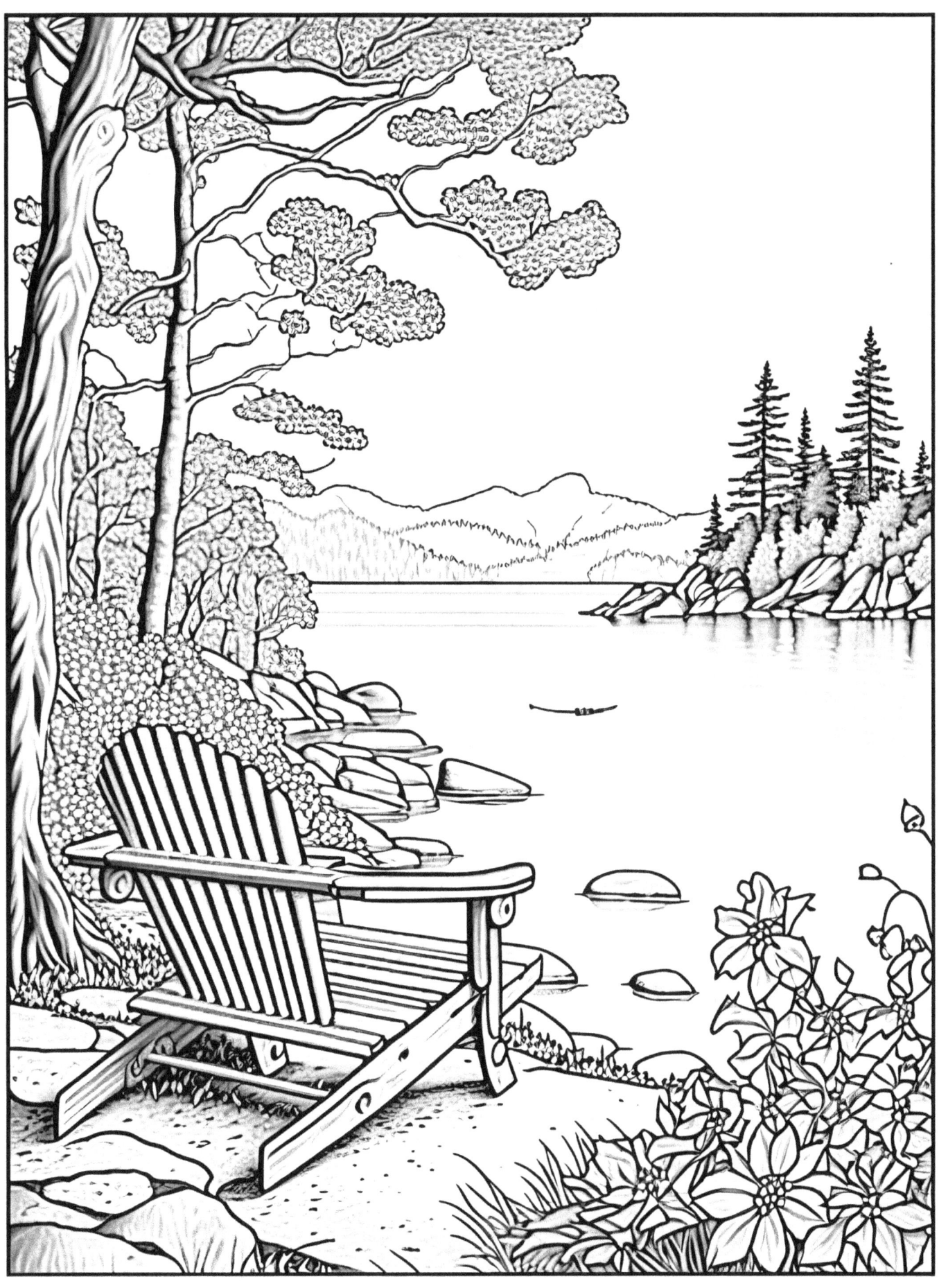

Farewell

As we reach the final page of this journey through idyllic retreats, may the serenity of these summer landscapes and the warmth of the inviting armchairs have brought you tranquility and inspired your creative spirit. The poems woven throughout this book were crafted to evoke the essence of each scene and provide a moment of reflection as you color.

We hope that each time you picked up your coloring tools and brought life to these images, you were transported to a world of relaxation and peaceful contemplation. Let the beauty of these summer havens linger in your heart and inspire you to create your own retreats in the days to come.

Thank you for joining us on this journey of color, poetry, and the joy of summer. May the memories of these idyllic retreats stay with you, and may you find peace and inspiration in every season of your life.

Get more Poem Coloring Books at:
www.pencil-playground.com